Inside the World Wide Web

"Coloured Bedtime StoryBook"

By

Roopa Pai

Illustrated by

Delwyn Remedios

ILLUSTRATED & PUBLISHED
BY
E-KİTAP PROJESİ & CHEAPEST BOOKS

www.cheapestboooks.com

 **www.facebook.com/EKitapProjesi**

ISBN: 978-625-6308-63-3

Copyright, 2024 by e-Kitap Projesi
Istanbul

Categories: Adventure, Community
Country of Origin: United States
Cover: © Cheapest Books
License: CC-BY-4.0

For full terms of use and attribution, http://creativecommons.org/licenses/by/4.0/

Contributing: Delwyn Remedios

© **All rights reserved**.

Except for the conditions stated in the License, no part of this book shall be reproduced or transmitted in any form or by any means, electronic or mechanical, including photocopy, recording or by any information or retrieval system, without written permission form the publisher.

About the Book

Know how to send an email? Of COURSE! Then you know what the internet is, don't you? Umm... sort of. And you know what www means, right? Welllll... kind of. You are feeling a little silly right now, aren't you? Mmmm. Never fear, Nettikutti is here! Gather round to listen as our bright little friend unravels the magic and mystery of the ginormous digital brain called the world wide web.

Have you heard of the World Wide Web? No?

Never mind.

Now, have you heard of the Internet? Yes? Great! But what IS the Internet? Did you say "I am not quite sure, but I know it has something to do with computers"? You're right - it does. But that's not the whole answer. What's the

WHOLE answer then? Hmmm. We need an EXPERT to answer that. And guess what - I know JUST the person! She's usually to be found near a computer, so let's go straight to the computer now.

Hi Nettikutti! Here is a group of kids to meet you! Come on out, come on out, wherever you are! THERE you are! Go on, kids, say hello! And don't be fooled by her cuteness and her size - she holds a LOT of information in her little head!

So Nettikutti, here's what everyone wants to know - what IS the Internet? Ooooh. BIG question. Let's see how I can put it simply. The Internet (short for 'INTERconnected NETworks') is a large, large, LARGE collection of computers from all over the world that are connected to each other.

The computers could be gigantic computers

(the kind research laboratories or governments

own), desktop computers (the kind you see in banks and computer centres), laptops (the kind people sling across their shoulders and carry with them), cellphones (the kind that ring so loudly and annoyingly in movie halls), and even the little music players with the itty-bitty headphones that seem to grow out of people's ears.

All these computers are connected with each

other either by real wires and cables - cables

that run above the ground, underground, even under the sea (big computers) - OR by wireless signals (laptops, cellphones, music players). So you see, you don't have to be sitting in one place and have your computer plugged into an electric socket to be on the Internet - you can even be connected to the world while you are on the move!

That's it? We thought the Internet was about talking to friends and downloading film songs and booking movie tickets and looking for information for school projects and finding the telephone number of a hospital! But that's not the Internet. All THAT is part of something truly magical, something called... wait for it.... the World Wide Web! This World Wide Web - let's call it W3 for short - is a large, large, LARGE collection of what are called PAGES (there are some 40 BILLION public pages on the W3 now!).

A page could contain information in the form of words, numbers, photographs, songs, video clips, and more. This collection of pages (or the W3) 'sits' on the Internet, in those millions of computers and cell phones and music players.

The Internet is a network of networks made up of computers, laptops, tablets and mobile phones. W3 is a collection of connected pages, that is on the Internet. So the W3 is NOT the Internet itself, but one PART of it, the coolest part. If you think of the Internet as a restaurant, then the W3 is the most popular dish on the menu. And the spoon that helps you dig into this dish and get to your favourite bits of it is called a 'Web Browser'.

Oooooh! Now you've made us hungry, Nettikutti! But do tell us more about what makes the W3 so popular. Sure! The W3 is super-exciting because it includes: Email - which allows you to send letters to anyone anywhere in the world - and have them receive it in under a minute! The same letter - if you were sending it to someone in America, say, would have taken 15 days to reach him if you had mailed it through a post office. And it would have cost you a lot of money too. But email is free!

Search - which helps you find useful - and useless! - information on a million different subjects. You may want to know which states the River Ganga flows through, or see what the Statue of Liberty looks like. You may want to hear the latest film song of your favourite actor, or watch an episode of a serial that you missed. You may want to find out the score in the T20 World Cup, or see if there are tickets available on the Mumbai-Pune train tomorrow. If someone whose computer is connected to the Internet, somewhere in the world, has decided to share this information with the world and put it on the W3, you will be able to find it - instantly! And for free!

But Nettikutti, HOW do you find the page that you want, out of all those billions of pages? Easy! Each page also has a unique 'address' which helps your Web Browser find it, just like your home address helps the postman to find your house. So if you know the page's address, you can go to it immediately. What if you don't know the page's address? No problem! You can use a wonderful service called a 'Search Engine', which also sits on the W3, to help you.

Sharing - which helps you share ANYTHING

you want - a song you love, your dog's picture,

a clever way to solve a difficult maths problem,

your big idea for keeping our streets free of

litter - with everyone in the world! No single

person owns the Internet or the W3, and no government has authority over it*, so you don't need to ask ANYONE for permission before you share. Think about how cool that is! Until now, you had books and movies and television and newspapers giving you information, 'talking' to you, but YOU couldn't talk back to THEM. With the W3, everything has changed - you can listen, and YOU CAN HAVE YOUR SAY too. And you don't have to be an important person or a grown-up to do this. THIS is what makes the w3 so fantastic - it is a truly free and open AND democratic system - it gives EVERYONE who is connected to the Internet a VOICE. *Governments do 'control' the internet in their own countries, however. Governments can even 'switch off' the internet, so that their citizens cannot access it, and some have actually done so for short or long periods.

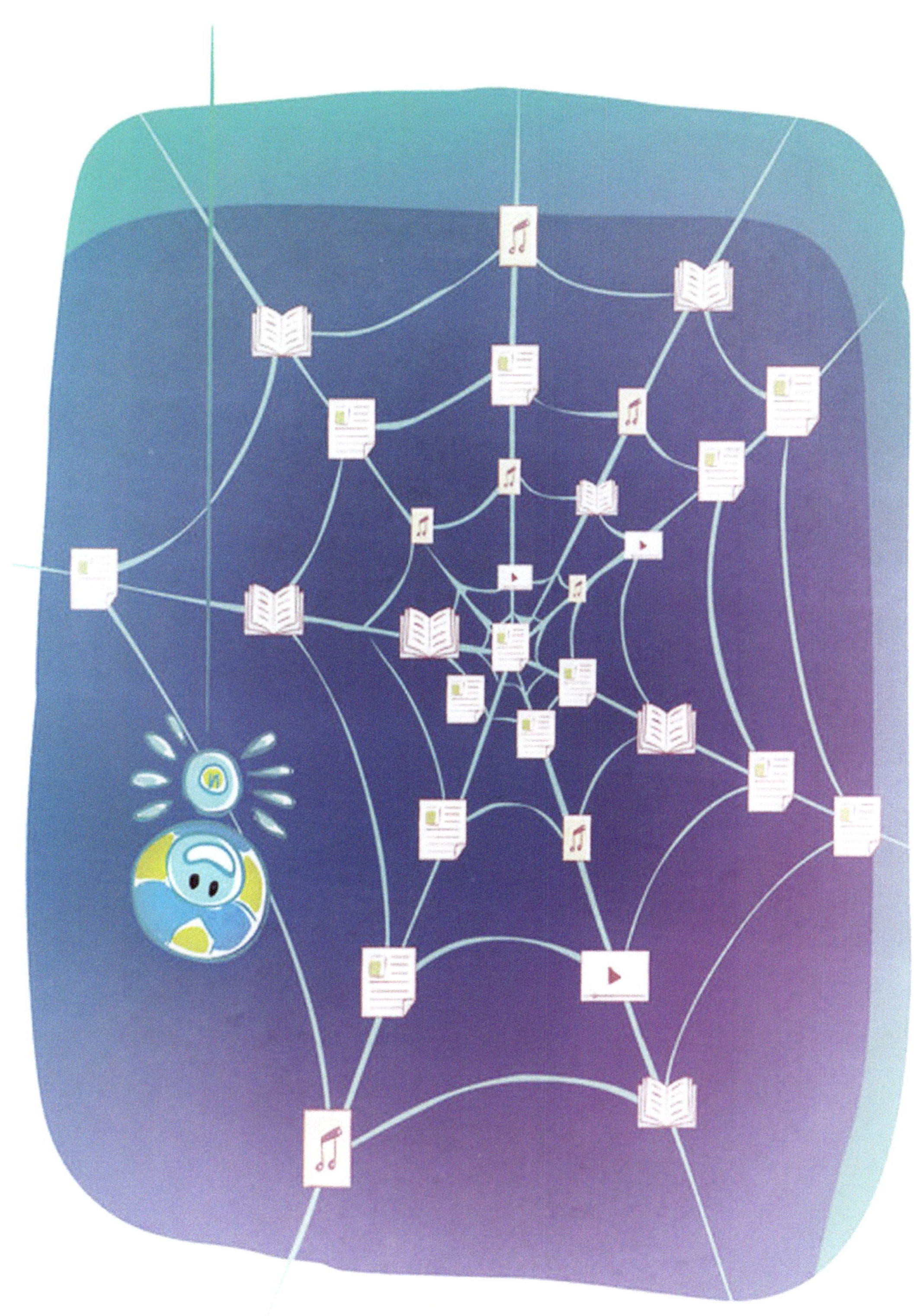

Wow! That's great, Nettikutti! Now, on a completely different tack - we understand why the first two Ws in W3 stand for World Wide, but why is it called a web? Isn't it the INTERNET that is actually a web? Good question! You're right about the Internet being a web (because of all those computers being connected to each other), but SO IS THE W3. Let me explain. Remember those billions of pages that the W3 is made of? THEY are all connected, or 'hyperlinked', to each other as well! That means you can go from one page to another almost endlessly! Do you see now how the W3 is ALSO a web, a HU-MUN-GOUS web of knowledge and information and entertainment for all humankind to enjoy and use?

We do, we do! Now we have to have to have to know - who was the superbrain who came up with such a wonderful idea? I thought you'd never ask! For the answer to that question, we have to go back in time some 20 years, to a nuclear research laboratory called CERN in Switzerland. Many scientists there, and across other labs in Europe, were working on projects together, but there was no way to share their work with each other quickly and easily. They would have to actually travel to each others' labs, or use the post office and courier services, to let their teams know how far they had progressed.

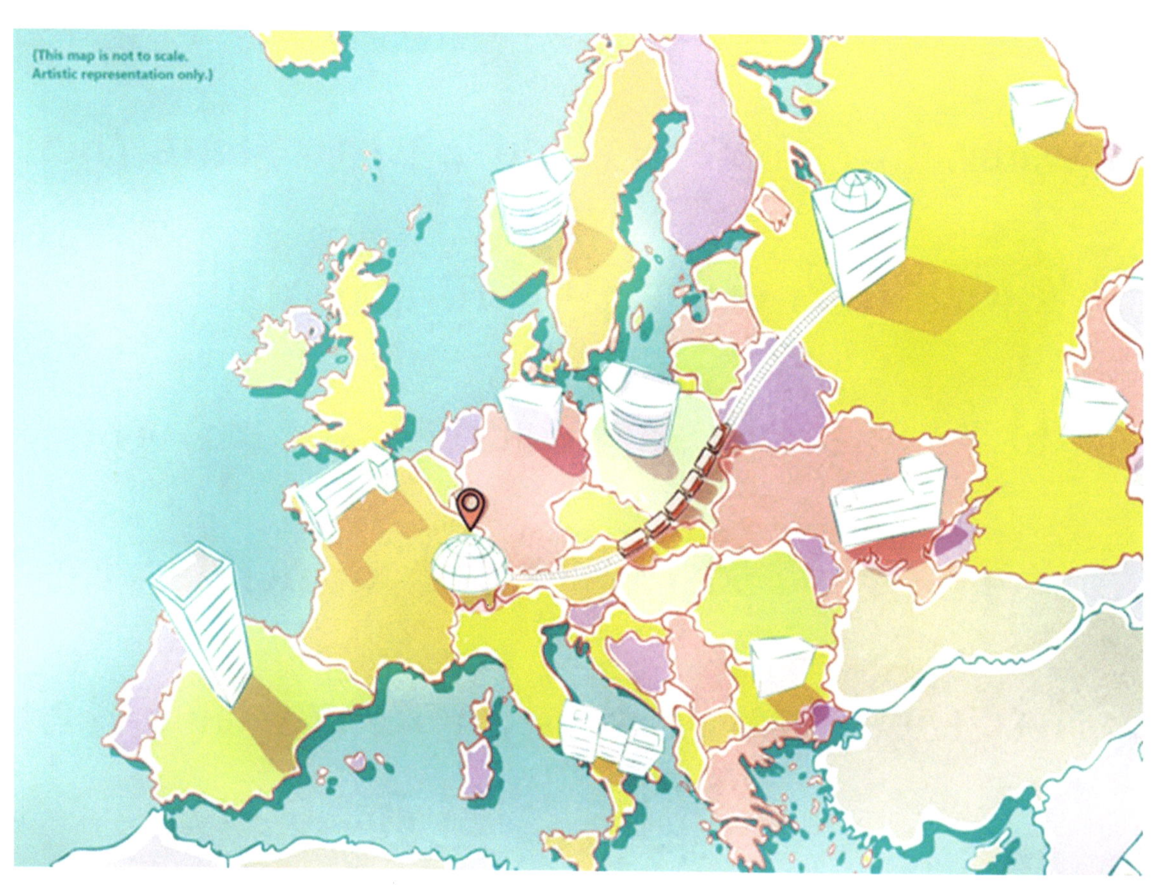

(This map is not to scale.
Artistic representation only.)

One of the scientists at CERN, Tim Berners-Lee, was getting a little fed up of this, so he decided to figure out a way to share information better and faster. He came up with a big idea called 'hypertext' - a way of linking information on computers together - to do this. The idea worked really well for CERN, and everyone was really happy. And THEN - Tim Berners-Lee had his SECOND big idea.

He felt his invention would benefit other people as well, and that it would be selfish to limit it to CERN. He talked to the authorities at CERN, and persuaded them to let him share the idea of hypertext with other scientists all over the world, for free. They agreed! Berners-Lee shared his idea, and urged everyone he shared it with to improve it or add to it as they wished. The idea of being able to access and share information from anywhere on earth instantly was SO powerful and SO attractive that a LOT of people began to use hypertext. Since anyone could use their own ideas to make it better, people all over the world felt they 'owned' the internet, that it was THEIRS. which was a wonderful thing.

By 1993, the W3 had EXPLODED, with millions of people beginning to use it. Today, more than TWO BILLION people use the W3 in some way - that is almost one-third of all the human beings on the planet! Hmmmm. Life would be very different today if Tim Berners-Lee had decided not to be so generous, right? Absolutely! So don't you think we should cheer both him and the W3 with a big Hip, Hip Hurray? We should! We should, Nettikutti! Here we go. To Berners-Lee and the W3 - Hip Hip... ...

HURRAYYYYYY!

End of the Story

www.ingramcontent.com/pod-product-compliance
Lightning Source LLC
LaVergne TN
LVHW071647180726
843512LV00002B/402